Great Answers to Difficult Questions about ADOPTION

WHAT CHILDREN NEED TO KNOW

Fanny Cohen Herlem

Jessica Kingsley Publishers
London and Philadelphia

This edition published in 2008
by Jessica Kingsley Publishers
116 Pentonville Road
London N1 9JB, UK
and
400 Market Street, Suite 400
Philadelphia, PA 19106, USA

www.jkp.com

First edition published in 2006 in French as L'adoption:
comment répondre aux questions des enfants

Copyright © Éditions Pascal 2006

Translated from French by Translate-A-Book, Oxford, England

All case histories and examples presented in the following are drawn from the author's
personal experience. Personal names have been changed to preserve confidentiality.

Library of Congress Cataloging in Publication Data

Herlem, Fanny Cohen.
  Great answers to difficult questions about adoption : what children need to know / Fanny
Cohen Herlem.
    p. cm.
  ISBN 978-1-84310-671-5 (pb : alk. paper)
  1. Adoption. 2. Adopted children. 3. Adoptive parents. 4. Questions and answers. I. Title.
HV875.H4165 2008
649'.145--dc22

                              2008007290

British Library Cataloguing in Publication Data
A CIP catalogue record for this book is available from the British Library

ISBN 978 1 84310 671 5

Printed and bound in Great Britain by
Athenaeum Press, Gateshead, Tyne and Wear

Preface

Adopt is a word derived from the Latin optare,
which means to choose, or to select.

The ancient practice of adoption has a varied history.
In Ancient Rome, for example, a father could elect to
accept or reject a child born to his wife. Once he
acknowledged the child, he would go on to "adopt"
him or her and bring the child up as his own legitimate offspring.

History and legend records the names of count-
less celebrated "adoptees", dating all the way back to
Moses, or Romulus and Remus. Examples of the
adoption process are frequent in literature and classi-
cal mythology. Most adopted children do not go on
to become famous, however, and the vast majority
are content to live out their lives in quiet anonymity.
Some are resolute in their determination to research
their own birth history, despite all the subsequent

complications and potential heartaches that it may sometimes entail.

Adoption is a hugely complex and sensitive subject area, and it prompts a wide range of fundamental questions about parenting. Accepting a child into a family implies a commitment to providing for his or her well-being, security, and intellectual and emotional development. In other words, the act of adoption assumes responsibility for a child's life, and especially for the way the child will fit within the family unit.

A sense of rejection

In any discussion of adoption, the notion of rejection or abandonment is never too far from the surface. Rejection often causes suffering not only for those who are rejected but also for those who do the rejecting. It is a notion that inevitably comes up sooner or later, most typically when an adopted child finally gets around to asking his or her new family when, how, by whom, and, not least, *why* he or she was "given up" or "abandoned". Questions such as these usually trigger others, some more direct, others more subtle. Try as they do to anticipate such questions, many parents are frequently ill-prepared and poorly equipped to respond. In part, this may be because questions tend to be asked at the most unexpected and awkward of moments – at the supermarket checkout, for instance, or waiting in a bus queue. I don't recall how many mothers have told me they scarcely had time to improvise some answer or other before the child had moved on to another subject entirely! At the same time, however, parents are understandably upset: they believe they have tried their best in all respects, but the child nevertheless still feels a deep-seated need to establish where he or she "comes from".

It is a common childhood fantasy that somewhere the child has a set of idealized parents, other than his or her own, and that perhaps those "real" parents are kings or queens so that he or she, by extension, must be a prince or a princess. This is an element of what Freud had in mind when he wrote about inventing a family "history". As it happens, however, the real parents of adopted children *are* genuinely different from the people who have brought them up. For a child, that reality is often difficult to accept. Children of any age, however young, crave certainty and truth. They need to discover and know things about themselves and their background in order to build a self-image on which they can build new memories and impressions. This is an essential part of growing up.

By the same token, adoptive parents have got to take account of things they don't or didn't know about their child, notably his or her experiences before the adoption, including feelings towards the biological parents. They have to decide how best to discuss this with the child and at what age. As a rule of thumb, it would seem important to talk these things through as soon as the child is old enough to ask such questions and to take in fully what is said in reply.

All children ask questions, adopted or not

Children understandably react to changing circumstances in their own lives and in the lives of those around them, and never more so than when a little brother or sister appears on the scene. In some cases, they will identify with these new arrivals, but in others, they will regard them as somehow "different" and have great difficulty in accepting them.

Children ask questions, and it is up to their parents to address those questions and to respond as truthfully as possible, albeit without going into more detail than is absolutely necessary. When a child asks where babies come from, for example, it is sufficient to give an answer suitable for the child's age and ability to comprehend. Over time, of course, a child's questions will gradually become more specific and more complex, and parents will have to respond as best they can.

The issue of adoption preoccupies the minds of lawmakers and lawyers, psychologists, children's rights activists, members of parent groups and associations, and, not least, it involves the full apparatus of the state. Accordingly, this book has one overriding objective, namely to help foster dialogue between parents and children and to facilitate frank and open discussion of a subject that is both complex and highly sensitive. It is hoped that the questions and answers drawn from real-life situations that are reproduced in the following short chapters will prove helpful to both parents and children. To all parents, however, a word of caution is in order: always keep in mind that you are parents first and foremost and that those asking the questions are, in the final analysis, only children!

Leo: A case in point

Leo was referred to me because he was experiencing difficulties at school: he was eight years old at the time. Leo and his twin brother were from an eastern European country, and they had been adopted at the age of two. While continuing to draw me a picture, he volunteered: *We're eight years old, and we're adopted.* I waited a moment before asking: "And how do you feel about that, being adopted?" Leo replied: *There was this lady, and there were seven or eight children, and then my mom came and they said to her, "Look, this one is Leo and this one is Julian" and that was all there was to it!*

Clearly, there is much that could be read into this brief exchange. Suffice it to say that it serves to illustrate to adults not only how a child might recount the story of his own life as it was told to him, but also how difficult it can be for a child to come to understand what it all means.

CHAPTER 1

Why was I abandoned: could it happen again?

It is perfectly natural to wonder what life may have been like for a child before he or she was adopted. Prospective parents can be forgiven for asking themselves if a child has been scarred in some way by his or her past and if old wounds will ever heal properly. They may even wonder whether the child will ever recover from the trauma and stress of having been given up for adoption. They will need to address the issues surrounding the child's biological parents.

Meanwhile, the child will be asking himself or herself other questions, perhaps including why he or she was rejected in the first instance. The child may recall details of life prior to adoption. It may sometimes be possible for adoptive parents to resurrect and incorporate certain elements from that former life, but the perennial problem is how best to do this, and when. Whatever they decide, parents should always try to respond as truthfully as possible to a child's questions.

Paul (9 years)

Why was I abandoned?

You've asked an important question. First of all, you know that it's never easy for a mom or a dad to give up a child. Very often, it is because they have no choice. In some countries, it may be because parents have other children and are unable or cannot afford to look after or even feed them all. It may be because the mom is a single parent, and the society where she lives won't accept her. In some cases, of course, parents may have deep-rooted personal reasons we can never know, but can only guess at.

But what about Emma? She was abandoned here in this country.

When that happens, there can be all kinds of reasons. Parents normally have to confirm that they are the biological parents, and to give their reasons for giving a child up for adoption. Not all of them do that – some because they don't know they should, and others probably because they just aren't prepared to make the effort.

Was I abandoned because I was naughty?

Certainly not! But you're not the first child to think that way – probably because rejection hurts so much and is very hard to understand. It's always difficult for us to accept that we're unwanted or perhaps even unloved and, as a result, we sometimes find it easier to blame ourselves.

Maybe it was because I was ugly as a baby?

If your birth mom decided she couldn't keep you, it was no doubt because she couldn't think what else to do. Maybe she was too young, or all on her own, or even in poor health. Who can say? But it's hard to believe that any mom anywhere would give a newborn baby up for no other reason than because it was ugly. Perhaps your "new" parents know more about this, so why not try asking them? There could be some explanation in a background file they were given, and I'm sure that you can count on them to share it with you.

Can my birth mom still take me back one day if she wants to?

No. Now that the adoption procedure has been completed – as in your case – your "new" parents are yours for life and no-one – absolutely no-one – can legally take you back.

But what will happen if I'm abandoned again?

A lot of adopted children secretly ask themselves that question.

So it's normal to worry about that?

Yes, it is. When you have been abandoned once already by your birth parents – for whatever reason – it's only normal to have problems trusting a new set of grown-ups, and to be afraid they might reject you if you do something silly. Adopted children often feel the need to put their new parents repeatedly to the test, because they are still confused about why they were abandoned in the first place. They may remain convinced it was because they misbehaved somehow. We've been through that already, and I hope I've set your mind at rest. But you should always remember that your new parents are there for the long haul, that they will stand by you and protect you all your life.

Anthony (8)

Every morning, I'm afraid to leave home for school. Why?

Let me try to explain. You love your home and you also love what it represents, namely your parents and family. It's understandable you don't want to leave home in the morning because you feel safe and secure there, surrounded by people who love you. And perhaps you are a little afraid you won't be able to find your way back there or that your parents will stop loving you when you're gone.

It's the same thing with my teacher. I'm afraid to leave school every afternoon...

You're absolutely right: it *is* the same thing. You feel safe around your teacher and every afternoon you don't want to leave school because you're scared she won't be there for you next morning. These fears are much more common than you'd think and the best way to get rid of them is to get them out in the open by talking about them. It's important to start believing in yourself, to see yourself as a person in your own right, with good points and bad.

How long will I be afraid like this?

Your fears will gradually disappear as family ties become stronger and as your family relationships develop. Your parents understand how being abandoned must have hurt, and they know how to react.

Nicholas (6)

What will happen to me if something bad happens to my new parents?

How do you mean?

Will I be put up for adoption again?

There's really no reason to worry that something bad will happen to your parents. And even if something serious were to happen to them, you can be sure that there are other members of their family – that's *your* family now, don't forget – who will be there for you.

Children are often afraid they will be abandoned and left alone again. There will always be some reason or other why they feel that way and it is up to parents to understand this and to be prepared to talk things through and set a child's mind at rest.

CHAPTER 2

Why have
my parents
chosen me?

Once a child has come to terms with the issue of being abandoned in the first place, his or her next question will almost certainly be why he or she was chosen in preference, say, to some other child who appears to be in exactly similar circumstances. "Why me?" is a question that parents need to address with great care. It is vital to offer reassurance to the child, but the question can also immediately prompt renewed anxiety about rejection, typically along such lines as: "If I don't behave, then these new parents will do what my first ones did, and simply give up on me."

Most adults will readily accept that a decision to adopt must never be taken lightly, but they should also understand that many of their concerns will be shared by the child. Age is a key issue: how old is the child and how old are any pre-existing brothers and sisters? Elements of the family "culture", such as likes and dislikes, joys and sorrows, and the ups and downs of day-to-day living are also important.

Underlying everything, there is always the problem of "choice". It is essential to explain to an adopted child that children are not simply selected at random from a number of "candidates". They are not "chosen" in the same arbitrary way as one might select an object, for instance, and this needs even more emphasis now that there is the possibility of adoption on the basis of a video or a website.

Amelia (7)

Why did my parents choose me?

There are many reasons why people wish to adopt a child. I suppose the most obvious reason of all is that they cannot have any children of their own. Or perhaps it's because they already have one child but would prefer to have one or two more and find they cannot – for medical reasons, for example.

I know all that, but why did they pick me?

Let me try to explain how it all works. First, you have to understand that it is not up to parents to "choose" a child. Instead, that is the responsibility of the people who make the arrangements for an adoption. They will carefully consider the parents' application and check their own files to see which set of parents might be best suited to a particular child. To that extent, they are the ones who do the choosing.

But how could they possibly have known?

For one thing, they knew you, or they had all your details on file. And then they carefully examined your parents' dossier to discover as much as they could about them: what they're like, how they live and so on. And finally they decided you were likely to be comfortable and happy with them as parents.

What about the children? Can they choose their new parents? Don't children have a say?

The short answer is "no". And, as far as choosing parents is concerned, I don't think that's a very good idea at all, any more than I believe parents should be allowed to choose their children!

Why isn't it such a good idea?

Because a person is not always what they seem or the way they are described. On first meeting, people can learn something about each other but not everything. It takes time to get to know and appreciate one another, and to get used to being a child to adoptive parents or parents to any particular child. In other words, there are no clear facts on which either the

parents or the child could base their selection. In the event, the question of "choice" doesn't come into it: once everything works itself out, I'm sure that your parents would find it impossible to imagine ever having wanted to be parents to any child but you!

I was a very young girl when I was adopted, but what if I were an older girl and didn't want to be adopted at all?

What you need to ask yourself is this: does this imaginary "older girl" of yours really mean it when she says she doesn't want to be adopted? Why might she say that? Is it because she wants to remain where she is, and not leave her friends or even her brothers and sisters behind? Perhaps she doesn't want to leave the country where she was born? Or maybe it's simply because she's worried about what the future may hold and whether she'll be able to handle it? Your question is a good one, but what it shows once again is how important it is for both children and parents to be thoroughly prepared for adoption. Anyway, once you have reached the age of thirteen, international law provides that you may not be put up for adoption unless you have been consulted.

Samuel (8)

My parents were still very young when they adopted me. Was that a good thing?

Yes, they were young when they adopted you, but the chances are that you were very young too! As for it being a "good thing", I don't think one can say either way. It may be important that adoptive parents appear to be parents rather than grandparents. I suppose all one can say is that it all comes down to the individuals involved.

Yes, I was still a baby! Is it better to adopt a baby than an older child?

I don't have a fixed answer to that. It all depends on how the parents feel about it. Some parents may prefer to adopt a small baby and watch him or her go through all the phases a child of their own would have gone through – crawling, starting to walk, learning to speak, and so on. I expect that was how it was with your parents. But, then again, there are other parents for whom that sort of thing is not as important, who are not so much into the baby phase, but who prefer to have a child with whom they can interact and share experiences.

But aren't babies much easier to deal with?

That may be true to the extent that they have spent less time in nurseries or other institutions. But just because they're tiny doesn't necessarily mean babies have not suffered or been exposed to emotional or even physical hardship and stress. They are too young to speak, so it can sometimes be hard to tell: there are only appearances. If they are lucky, and are adopted by considerate parents like yours, however, they soon respond and adapt.

Many people don't realize that, although the rules may vary from one country to the next, babies can't normally be put up for adoption before the age of two or three months. In developed countries, babies that are up for adoption are usually placed in care as of the day they are born. In poorer countries this may not be the case, and babies may be denied proper medical care and attention, even if the people who are responsible for them do the best they can.

But what about you? Do you remember being adopted?

No, because I was so tiny! I suppose someone older would probably remember a lot more.

It is often said that older children find adoption more difficult to handle because they've been through a lot more. That may well be true but they are also old enough to talk about the past, to put into words their likes and dislikes, and to share their hopes and fears. They are often so happy to be part of a family where they can bond and settle that any problems they may have tend to be minor.

I would say that successful adoption is less a question of age than a question of what parents are looking for in a child and how well they prepare themselves to meet that child's needs.

Jemma (8)

My dad says I didn't have brothers or sisters, but what would have happened if there had been several of us?

As a matter of principle, when several children from the same family are placed in an institution or in foster care, they should be kept together and never separated. On the other hand, it can sometimes happen that an abandoned child has brothers or sisters about whom nothing is known at the time. When a child is older, he or she may start to remember and then try to find these brothers and sisters. Sadly that is seldom an easy thing to do.

Yes, I suppose that must be hard – and you'd always keep asking yourself why me and not my brother.

It is often the case that the child who has been abandoned will ask why it happened to him or her and not to the others. Since there's usually no way of knowing why, a child can take it very badly.

But look at it another way: now that you do have a big brother, you probably realize that it's not just having the same parents that makes you brother and sister. It's also the fact that the two of you were brought up together under the same roof and that you have so much of your past in common. In other words, adopted children have brothers and sisters even when their birth parents are different. In fact, just like natural brothers and sisters, they are not allowed to marry one another.

CHAPTER 3

How did my parents adopt me?

Children are naturally inquisitive. Even when they've heard their story, they often like to hear it over and over again. This is partly because, as they get older, their perspective on life changes and they feel the need to ask different questions, or in a different way. Those questions will mostly be about themselves, but they will also be about their adoptive parents. For one thing, it is very important to children – especially as they get older – to understand what adoption is and what it involves, not least because it all sounds so complicated when grown-ups discuss it. Their need to know may be even greater when friends and others start asking questions, or if they meet other adopted children, perhaps from other countries or different situations.

Accordingly, patiently explaining the ins and outs of the adoption process in some detail is an important step in helping a child understand his or her own story. It also helps to underline a key message, namely that adoption must never be about finding the right child for a family but, instead, should always be about finding the right family for the child.

Bernard (7)

Where have adopted children come from?

The children usually live in nurseries when they are very young, or with foster parents or in orphanages when they are older.

Mom says I came from a nursery. Is that true?

Yes. You were just a baby when your parents saw you for the first time.

But how did my parents know they were allowed to adopt me?

Your parents had decided they wanted to adopt a child, so they went to see the people who are in charge of adoption in your country. They were told that all your papers were in order and that you were available for adoption, because you had no legal parents.

What did they do then?

They had already been sent your photo and some details about you. They must have liked what they saw and read! Why don't you ask them about that one of these days? Then they had to make up their minds on a couple of things. For example: would they prefer to adopt a very young child or one who was a little older? Did they want a child born in this country or abroad?

Did they have to say if they wanted a little boy or a little girl?

Perhaps they did, perhaps they didn't. In most cases, parents don't seem to mind: they want to adopt a child and it doesn't really matter to them whether it's a boy or a girl. There are times when people say they prefer one or the other, but that's often for a very simple reason – perhaps they would prefer a little girl because there are already a number of boys in the family or vice versa. And sometimes they will say that they prefer a little boy (or a little girl) because they think boys (or girls) are easier or even more fun to bring up!

Can every adult adopt a child?

Certainly not! It's much more complicated than that!

First of all, your parents had to be given permission to adopt you. That meant meeting people and telling them all about themselves and waiting to see if they were allowed to adopt you.

Parents who wish to adopt a child born abroad would normally make arrangements to travel directly to the country and work with an intermediary organization that can advise them throughout the process. A child must be declared legally available for adoption by an appropriate authority in that country.

Steven (11)

Why did my parents want a child from my country?

There could be all sorts of reasons for that. Sometimes, parents choose a particular country because they have spent time there and they are fond of the people. That was maybe what happened with your parents. Sometimes, people have family connections with a country, perhaps they or their own parents were born there. Often, there are simply not enough children available for adoption in their own country.

Does that mean they would have preferred to adopt a boy born in this country?

I don't believe that for an instant. I'm sure your parents were simply anxious to adopt a child – period! All they wanted was to become parents! It did not matter to them where the child was from. Then you came along, and their wish was granted!

Who finally decided they could adopt me?

That decision was taken by a number of people working together with your parents, including child psychologists and other professionals, who are familiar with and trained in all aspects of adoption.

In other words my parents had to pass an examination?

You could say something like that. You see, not everybody can adopt a child, even if they are really nice. Besides, not every child is available for adoption!

So how did it all work?

There were a lot of steps to be followed in both countries. Every country has its own laws and regulations with respect to adoption and your parents had to obey those laws and regulations to the letter. That is probably why some people complain that adoption is such a complicated and long drawn-out process. Most people understand that the laws are there to protect both the children and the adoptive parents.

What do you mean when you say adopted children are protected?

They are protected in all sorts of different ways. For example, there are laws to prevent children being bought or sold once their birth parents are no longer in a position to care for them and have entrusted them to a special home or a similar institution. Additionally, most countries have officials to make sure that the adoptive parents are suitable. They may decide, for example, that the very youngest children are to be entrusted only to younger parents. In some countries there is even a rule that adoption is not permitted to parents who already have natural children of their own.

Alan (11)

My parents always say it takes two to adopt.

That's not necessarily true. An individual may wish to adopt in certain instances, but it all depends on the laws of the country concerned. In some countries a single person of either sex requires special permission to adopt, whereas in others it is forbidden outright. In a few countries, provision can even be made for a child to be adopted by an unmarried man.

Why is it like that?

I think it's fair to say that adoption is more complicated for a single person. What is certainly true is that a single mom (or, indeed, a single dad) can prove a loving and attentive parent. But having both a dad and a mom is usually best for a child's development.

But some of my friends say they never see their dad and my friend Mark even says he doesn't have a dad!

Come on, those two things aren't the same, are they? It's one thing to know you have a dad you never see, and another thing entirely to say you have no dad at all. Let's face it, everyone had to have a dad – at one point, biologically speaking, he was just as important as your mom. Obviously, everything is easier when there are two parents who can help one another to take turns and share responsibilities. For the adopted child it's like being born into a whole new family again.

Jennifer (10)

Is it true that you have to buy adopted children?

What a strange question to ask!

Aurelia once said that Sarah's parents bought her in the country where she was born.

The fact is that under international law it is strictly forbidden to buy or sell a human being. What that means is that no person can *ever* legally sell a child simply because he or she needs the money, and no person can *ever* buy a child just because they want one. I think it's best if you discuss this with your parents, and they will be able to tell you exactly what happened in your case, for example.

But why would Aurelia have said something like that?

All I can think of is that she maybe heard someone say it can be expensive adopting a child from another country.

You see! My friend Aurelia was right after all! You do have to pay for adopted children!

No, that's not the way it is at all!

Certainly, there may be some expense, but it's not the *child* that costs money, it's the adoption process itself.

For a child to be declared legally abandoned and available for adoption, all kinds of people are involved, including lawyers, court interpreters, certified translators, and others, because every detail has to be recorded for the benefit of the judge. Their services cost money. Those are what are known as "administrative costs" and that's the expense we're talking about. What can also happen in some cases is that parents will make a financial contribution to the institution or home where the child lived up until the adoption – donating money is one way of helping the other children living there. Parents will have done their sums in advance, of course, so they should have provided for these costs and none of it should come as a surprise, assuming everything is above board.

What do you mean: "above board"?
That means that everything is done legally and that people are honest.

But I've heard there is an illegal market in adopted children. Is that true?
Yes, that is unfortunately true. Illegal trafficking does exist and parents who intend adopting in a foreign country have to be very cautious indeed, because nothing could be worse than suddenly being told they are expected to pay to adopt the child who has been assigned to them. There is also a danger that a child later comes to believe – wrongly – that he or she is with a particular set of parents purely as the result of a financial transaction, and that would be horrible, don't you think?

Yes, it would!

CHAPTER 4

We're a family now – just like other people!

To be adopted is to become part of a family. But what does the word "family" really mean? In a sense, a family is a sort of "home port": a safe haven to which one can return time and again. It also implies a network of lifelong relationships: parents, grandparents, uncles, aunts, and so on.

Adoptive parents normally feel a keen sense of anticipation before the "child of their dreams" finally arrives, and once he or she has arrived, they will do whatever they can to make the child feel at home in the fullest sense. They will begin to pass on to the child certain "family values" they themselves have inherited from preceding generations. In this way, a sense of continuity is gradually built and another link is forged in the chain of family history. This process of acceptance and integration applies even if several children are adopted, irrespective of whether or not the family has other "biological" children.

Kahlea (9)

I don't remember meeting my parents for the first time. What was it like?

I don't know, so I'm not the person to ask: it's best to ask your parents.

What I *can* tell you is that every parent I have ever met and spoken with over the years has always described that first encounter as a very moving experience. After all, everyone involved has been on "hold" for months on end, waiting for the big day when all the formalities of adoption are completed. If the adopted child is very young, of course, he or she cannot be expected to appreciate fully what is going on. In the case of older children, I suppose the dominant feeling is best described as a sense of nervous anticipation.

Why "nervous"?

Isn't that obvious? Just think about it: everyone involved – parents and children alike – is worried about how things will work out. How will the child react? How will the parents respond? Will they hit it off right away? Or will it take some time to get used to one another? And, if so, how much time?

What I don't get is how they recognize one another?

If, like you, the child is from another country, the future parents will have been sent some photographs. They will have a photo of you and you will have been given a photo of them. To them, you are already a familiar face and they will have no problem recognizing *their* child.

What if I'd been born in this country?

I imagine that might have made things even easier. Your parents would probably have been to visit you several times already and, by the time of adoption, you would all have had plenty of time to get to know one another.

Kate (8)

I'm going to have a little sister one day soon. Her name is Cora and she's from a country called Bulgaria. Our whole family can hardly wait.

And what about you? Are you looking forward to her arrival?

I think there's maybe been too much fuss about it! There are photos of her all over the house and she's all we ever talk about!

Do you think you might be just a teensy bit jealous?

What if I am? I'll have to share my room with her. She doesn't even speak English! And she's three years old already!

I understand. I see that it's hard for you to accept a little girl coming here as your new sister. Especially since she wasn't born in this country and you've had no chance to watch and get used to her as she grew up. But why don't you put yourself in her shoes?

Try to imagine how hard it must be for her, not just coming to a different country, but then finding out she'll be spending her days with a big sister she doesn't know anything about.

It'll take time to get to know one another, but you'll both have to accept that.

Do you think Cora should be told she's adopted?

I most certainly do! I also believe she already knows.

How could she? At her age?

I know she's very young, but your parents think she's old enough to understand.

But why tell her at all?

Because it's important always to tell children the truth and because there's no time like the present! It's not too soon to tell Cora that her mom and dad are not her birth parents. Besides, don't you think Cora already knows deep down that she was abandoned as a very young child, that she has now exchanged one mom for another?

More important, to my mind, is not *when* to tell Cora but *how* to tell her. Your parents – and good parents everywhere – already know there is more to having children than the simple act of bringing them physically into this world. Parenting is about caring and nurturing, about loving a child and helping that child to grow and develop into adulthood. It is about telling the child that they are wanted as clearly and as often as possible, irrespective of how old he or she is. As you know, children need to hear the truth – otherwise how can we ever expect them to trust a grown-up? Believe me, your little sister Cora is no exception.

So, when should she be told?

There is no simple answer to that. It's up to your parents to decide when the time is right, both for them and for Cora. Even then, it's not simply a question of "getting something off your chest" once and for all: this is a subject that is bound to come up time and again.

Mom says adopted children know they're adopted without being told. Is that true?

What and how much they know will obviously depend on how old they were at the time of adoption. They may or may not remember specific things, or they may or may not be able to describe what they remember in any great detail. There may be certain smells or tastes, perhaps, or distinct or vague images that they can't quite place. Some children may remember places where they once lived or, if they are old enough, people who took care of them at one time or another. When this happens, it's never helpful to suggest they are too young and can't possibly remember or to say they are "imagining" things. Instead, it is important to try to explain what these memories mean and how they fit together.

But don't you think it would upset Cora to talk about stuff like that?

It's hard to say. It might upset her to be reminded of certain people, places and events – her birth parents, for instance, or the fact of being abandoned – but it should always be possible to talk about things, whatever her age. In Cora's case, it is important for you all to try to learn as much as you can about her – perhaps there's some additional information in her file that could prove useful.

It's all getting too complicated! I'm beginning to think I'd prefer not to have a little sister!

Now, now! Let me ask you this: do you genuinely think that any child – adopted or otherwise – should have the right to decide there should be no other children in the family? Once you have brothers and sisters, you have to learn to share your parents' love and attention, but you must know by now that your parents love you and are capable of enough love to go around all their children. Don't forget: they thought long and hard before they decided to adopt another child, and they also discussed that step with you – the big sister – to discover how you felt about it. Perhaps you didn't make your feelings sufficiently clear.

But what if they'd decided to adopt someone older than me?
How would you have felt about that?

I wouldn't have been happy if someone had taken my place.
I'm still the oldest child in the family and I want it to stay
that way!

That only goes to show how important it is for everyone to sit down together and talk things through. Every new addition to the family has to find his or her place and it is up to the other members of the family to accept the new set-up and be comfortable with it. If the new arrival has to be "slotted in" between two brothers or sisters, things may prove a little awkward, but only at first – it will soon pass.

It won't be easy for Cora to fit in. It's not as if Mom
actually carried her in her tummy all this time.

Don't forget that your parents have already made room for her in your lives. And, when Cora finally arrives, she and they – and you, too – will soon adjust and get used to her being around. And you can help her settle in – by teaching her things and passing on what you know. She doesn't know how lucky she is, having a big sister like you!

Family Tree

In school, children are sometimes encouraged to volunteer details about their family and home life, or to draw a family tree, or bring family photos to class. This can prove difficult and potentially embarrassing for some children, but it is a situation that often cannot be avoided. Eight-year-old Leo – whom we met earlier – explained to me one day how he had handled it: *I drew a family tree with the names of my dad and mom at the top, together with those of my brothers and sisters: then I put my own name above them all and off to one side. I drew a speech balloon with the name of the country*

where I was born and then used a dotted line to join up the balloon and my own name. I thought this up all by myself and I was really proud when I showed my parents.

Enough said!

CHAPTER 5

Everyone says I'm different!

Among the awkward questions parents and adopted children may one day have to field, none is perhaps more intrusive than why there is no immediate and striking resemblance between members of the same family. Putting aside the question of whether members of a family should necessarily look like one another in order to be considered part of the same family, this also illustrates the problem some people have in imagining family relationships other than those of a biological nature.

Typically, parents of adopted children will have anticipated this type of question and will be ready to respond, asserting their parental status in no uncertain terms. Questions such as this may often unsettle an adopted child, however, and it is important that parents lead by setting an example and demonstrating how best to deal simply and effectively with such questions. Their approach will also help any other children in the family to come to terms with adoption generally and the questions it raises.

Jade (8)

Some of the children at my new school say my Mom isn't my real mom because I don't look a bit like her!

How do you feel about that?

It made me angry at first, but then it made me feel so sad that I didn't want to talk about it any more.

But you can't get it out of your mind? Is that it?

I suppose so. You see, I was born in China. I have jet-black hair, but my parents are both blond!

And you think that should be enough for other children to start saying your Mom isn't your real mom?

No, I don't think so. But why don't they believe me?

Just because you don't physically resemble your parents, these other children seem to have a major problem understanding that the two grown-ups you live with are your mom and dad. What that tells me is that those children have been taught nothing about adoption, and it's high time someone taught them. Why not tell your parents and ask them to speak to your teacher?

Do you think the children will listen to what the teacher says about it?

Why not? Children usually pay attention to what their teacher says! But what seems much more important to me is that you should keep insisting that your Mom and Dad are your parents, whether you look like them or not! Being parents and children, a family, is about so much more than simply looking like one another!

Reuben (13)

Mom and I were out shopping the other day when a lady stopped and asked us where we were from. She was quite polite about it, I suppose, but it really bugged me.

What did your mom reply?

She asked the lady why she wanted to know.

And then?

She looked sort of embarrassed, but then she asked my mom if we were really her children, because she'd heard us calling her "Mom". Then my mom just looked her straight in the eye and she said – and she was really cool – "Yes, they're mine!"

What do you make of that?

I reckon we didn't ask her where she came from! I also think she should mind her own business. And let us get on with our life!

There's no getting away from it: it was rude of that woman to comment on physical differences between children and their mom. Sadly, adults can sometimes be like that, but don't forget: when someone asks that kind of question, you're not obliged to react at all, let alone reply.

Zoe (11)

A few days back, my mom, my brother, and I were in a movie queue when this couple started looking at us – really looking. All of a sudden, the woman turned to Mom and said something like "the little boy looks pretty much like you, but I suppose the little girl must take after her dad?" Can you believe it?

How did you react to that?

How do you think? I blew my top. What really gets me is that I want so much to look like my mom, because I think she's gorgeous! But I don't suppose I'll ever get to be like her.

Why not?

Because I don't have skin like hers. Hers is really white whereas mine is darker. And because my hair is all curls and hers is straight!

What does your mom say about that? Or your dad?

They both say I'm very pretty and my dad says I've got loads of personality, just like my mom!

There! It so happens you're like your mom, after all: not in looks, maybe, but in personality. And don't you think that's every bit as good?

Julian (9)

I got into a fight at school this morning because some boys were making fun of my brother Silvio, who's only four years old. They were teasing him because he's a different color from them!

I think you did the right thing, sticking up for him like that! The fact is that some children seem to have a problem accepting anyone who is a bit different. It needs to be explained to them – one way or another!

They keep saying he's not my brother because he's adopted!

That's only because they don't fully understand what "being adopted" really means. As far as you're concerned, he *is* your little brother: he has the same family name as you and you have the same parents. The only difference is that you came into the family at birth whereas he came along later. But the fact that you have so many things in common makes you brothers. You simply have to accept that this is sometimes too difficult for some children to take in at first.

What about Silvio? Will he end up looking like me?

Who does someone look like? Now there's a question that keeps coming up time and again! It seems it's something we're all interested in. Until a baby is born, it doesn't really matter all that much how we pictured him or her in our mind's eye or how much we looked forward to the birth. It is only when he or she actually comes into this world that we're confronted by this tiny new human being who is both familiar and, at the same time, an unknown quantity. The baby may be "familiar" for all sorts of reasons: to the mom, perhaps, because she has felt the baby shift and grow in the womb, or to both parents who may have already seen and "met" the child via an ultrasound scan. He or she may also be an "unknown quantity" quite simply because every human being is unique, a "one-off" unlike any other.

Okay, but there you're talking about babies with natural parents, just like me.

As it happens, it isn't all that different in the case of an adopted child. His or her arrival on the scene has also been eagerly anticipated and his or her physical appearance may also have been captured on camera. But once he or she finally arrives, we're talking about a real person in his or her own right, someone we have to get to know.

That doesn't answer my question.

Trust me, I'm getting there! You've probably heard it said that a baby "takes after" his or her mom or dad or even an uncle, aunt, or grandparent, perhaps because they have "the same" eyes or "the same" pointed ears or "the same" long and delicate fingers. Those similarities are, of course, purely physical. But, over time, other traits come into play, in terms of personality. That's why we say things like: "He's stubborn, just like his dad", or "She's impatient, just like her Aunt Ethel", or "He has Uncle Pete's temper".

What I'm saying is that there are all sorts of different ways of being "like" someone – not only physically but also in terms of temperament. Children *and* parents come to resemble each other by developing as a family unit. One day, I'm sure, you'll see that for yourself.

Yes, but the fact remains that Silvio is different – he's adopted!

I agree. In Silvio's case, physical likeness will be less pronounced – that's only to be expected, after all – although I've known cases of children growing up to look increasingly (and almost inexplicably) like their adoptive parents or other family members. I remember one instance in particular. I saw a photograph of a little African girl with her adoptive grandmom. Both of them had their mouths wide open, laughing fit to bust, and I was immediately struck by how alike they were. One was the spitting image of the other! It just goes to show how a common identity can evolve, as one member of a family unwittingly imitates another.

How does that work?

Family likenesses develop because of how and what parents or other members of the family communicate to a child, and the way that the child assimilates and responds to those influences. Thus, a child might develop the mom's love of horses, for example, or turn out to be as serious-minded and studious as a big brother or, for that matter, as scatterbrained as a favorite aunt! The simple fact is that we tend to take on characteristics of family members we particularly love and admire. Of course, there is a world of difference between being "like" someone and being "identical" with that person, and none of this means that we are somehow less of an individual in our own right.

But Silvio keeps looking at himself in the mirror and asking me if he looks like his birth dad or mom?

It's normal to want to know that, and it's complicated if your parents don't have a photo of Silvio's birth parents (which is often the case) so that he can never be given a satisfactory answer to his question. But it's important for him, and for you, to remember that there's so much more to identity than mere physical resemblance.

In other words, he'll never know who he'll look like when he grows up? I mean to say, when I look at my dad, I just know I'll grow up to look pretty much like him one day!

Sure, you'll probably look something like your dad, but I bet there'll be your mom's looks in there, too, and even something of great grandparents – people you've never even met but have maybe only ever seen in photos. You and I are fortunate enough to know that physical resemblance is not what it's all about. But it can be very hurtful for a child or a teenager not to know what his birth parents looked like: the color of their hair, for example, or their eyes. As an adopted child, this is something Silvio will have to learn to live with. Over time, however, you'll find that your little brother will start to take on certain features of your parents; he'll "adopt" some of their gestures and mannerisms, for example, or share their likes and dislikes. And, because he likes you and looks up to you as his big brother, Silvio will no doubt also start doing some things *your* way.

Alice (12)

My friend Sarah is black, but her parents are white. That's kind of weird, isn't it?

I wouldn't call that "weird" – that's going too far, don't you think? After all, you know Sarah was born in Africa, that her birth mom was African and that she was adopted!

Yes, but does Sarah know?

I believe she does. And not just because her skin is a different color, but because her parents will have told her.

With some children, you'd never know they were adopted just by looking at them!

Because they look like their parents, you mean?

Yes.

Well, perhaps the parents deliberately adopted a child they thought would grow up to look as much like them as possible, a child from a country where people are physically not so very different from them.

— *CHAPTER 6* —

Where does my first name come from?

One question that often arises among adoptive parents is whether or not they should change the child's given name. It can only be answered satisfactorily once other issues have been thought about.

A child's first, or "given", name can be an important part of his or her identity. It follows that parents anxious to change the given name of an adopted child should first ask themselves why and on what basis. Is it the intention – as is often the case – to bind the child more closely into his or her new family, by using, for example, the same first name as a cherished grandparent, a favorite uncle or aunt, or a close family friend?

A child's given name is in all likelihood the one chosen by his or her biological parents or, failing that, the name by which he or she came to be known on a day-to-day basis in the country of origin. It is the name most closely associated with the child, and, clearly, should not be changed arbitrarily.

The importance of a child's given name will vary depending on the age of the child concerned. A name change may be of little concern to a very young child, but may be extremely important to one who is significantly older. Ultimately, it is commonly accepted that, irrespective of their age, children typically want to have been named by their parents, and to have a given name not unlike that of most other children in the country of their adoption. In other words, they prefer to have a name that does not set them immediately apart as "different".

Jamie (8; originally José, from Bolivia)

Why do I have two first names now? An English one and a Spanish one?

Well, you were born in a Spanish-speaking country and, like all the other children there, you had a Spanish name – which was probably chosen by your birth parents. Then, when your new parents adopted you, they thought it might be best to keep your Spanish name and give you another English-language first name, like theirs.

Yes, I suppose. But our school is full of children who don't have English first names.

Does that really matter to them, or to anyone else?

But it's not the same thing. Those children live with their real parents, so if the parents are from a foreign country, they have a name from that country.

When you first arrived in this country, your parents wanted to give you a new first name as a way of helping you settle into your new family. I expect that they also thought it was important to you to keep the first name you had before, the name you had in the country where you were born.

Now, I'm okay with "Jamie". I suppose it's better than the really far-out names some of the children at school have.

Yes, it's true that there are some given names that are almost impossible to pronounce. It is also true that some of them are probably very beautiful names in their country of origin, but sound funny or less attractive here in this country. But you have to remember that we live in a country which has people from almost every part of the world, so we are already used to names that sound unusual to us!

The big difference is that the children with the far-out names also have parents with weird names!

That's how it is for them, because the whole family is from another culture.

Maybe later, once I'm older, I can decide to call myself anything I want?

Right now, you seem to be perfectly happy with "Jamie", but later, if you prefer to use your other first name and call yourself "José", that's up to you. Why shouldn't you? But, there again, why *should* you?

Do you have to change your given name when you're adopted?

No. In fact the original name is often kept, particularly when the child in question is older. Can you imagine what that would be like, otherwise? Being known by one name for years on end and then suddenly being called by a completely different one? That's enough to confuse anyone.

In some cases, parents will change a first name slightly, in order to adapt it to more common usage in their home country, say "Joseph" instead of "José". In my experience, however, most parents tend to choose a new first name for an adopted child *and* also retain the child's original name.

Just as you said, an older child may prefer to choose to be known by a single name – either the first name given to him at birth or solely by his "new" name.

Does that mean I'd have been free to choose my own name if I'd been old enough when I was adopted?

Not really. As a general rule, it is up to the adults to name their children. But, as we said earlier, children – adopted or otherwise – can at some point, later in life, decide to call themselves by one or other of their given names.

Well, that's like my friend Ernesto: he wants people to call him by his second name, Vincent, because that's the name of one of his new uncles who plays great piano! And Ernesto is dead set on becoming a jazz musician when he's older!

That's why a given name is often so important: it can help identify with a person of the same name.

So he can keep both names, if he wants?

Yes, and that way he can show respect for his natural parents who chose his original given name, and for the country where he was born, but also for his new parents. That will mean a lot to them.

— CHAPTER 7 —

Who were
my parents when
I was born?

Some adopted children remain torn between their biological parents, and sometimes their country of birth, on the one hand and, on the other, their "new" parents. In other words, their loyalties are effectively divided between their "roots" and their new life within their adoptive family.

Adoptive parents may feel uncomfortable or even apprehensive when an adopted child starts asking questions about his or her "other" parents or "my parents from before". Even so, they should never duck the issue. Instead, they should see it as an opportunity to review the common history – the sequence of events that brought them together with the child. Exploring this story can go some considerable way towards allaying a child's worst fears – not to mention any uncertainty and insecurity the parents may feel themselves.

Adoptive parents need to be cautious when they reply to questions about biological parents. For a start, it is vital to reassure the child that the adoption was lawful, and that his or her biological parents were aware of – and prepared to accept – the consequences. At the same time they should explain that records and files never tell the whole story, and that there is no way to be sure how biological parents may have felt at the time, or what was going through their minds prior to giving up their child.

In some instances, of course, there may be almost no information available about a child's past life – in which case, the chances are that the child will invent an imaginary one. Parents can and should help by providing as much constructive input as they possibly can, and by stressing how happy they were at the prospect of welcoming a new addition to their family.

Sebastian (14; originally from Ecuador)

What will happen if I want to see my real parents again?

First, you should think about why you feel this need. You need to know why because, generally speaking, the actual search process takes a long time and is far from simple. I don't doubt you have your reasons, and that they are perfectly valid – all I'm saying is that you have to be very clear in your own mind as to what you really want, how much time it may take, and how disappointing the outcome may eventually be.

How difficult will it be to find them?

It's not always possible to trace birth parents, and it tends to be even more difficult in the case of children born in a foreign country. An obvious first step is to visit the country to see what official records are available, and find out if you are entitled to access them. You could also try to get in touch with people who might have known your biological parents. However you look at it, there's a lot of detective work involved.

What about my friend Philip? He was born in this country, so is it easier?

Yes, that might make things easier. In this country it is possible – assuming the present whereabouts of one's birth parents are known – to contact them through an official agency to find out if they will agree to a meeting.

You say it's difficult for me, but some children do manage to track down their birth parents, don't they?

Yes, and I've heard a lot of stories. There are mixed results, I should say. In some cases, everything worked out well, but in others the outcome was far from happy. Some reunions were joyous affairs, others not. Some people stayed in contact afterwards, others did not.

Why was that?

Every story is different. Some children merely wanted to see who and where their birth parents were, and were content to leave it at that. Others reacted in different ways: some were disappointed and some were surprised – favorably or otherwise – when they found themselves face to face with these strangers, people with whom they appeared to have little or nothing in common. Some were simply delighted.

Do you think it would be better simply to find out all about them without actually meeting them face to face?

Let's just say you have every right to know the facts about your own life, however pleasant or unpleasant those may be. My feeling is that it is best not to face such things alone, but to have someone there to talk to, to confide in. This person may or may not be one of your parents.

Angela (12)

Can someone have two dads and two moms?

On balance, I'd have to say the short answer to that question must be "no".

You mean it's impossible?

Let's talk this through. Your biological – "birth" – parents got together and had a child, and that was you. We all have biological parents, of course, but it sometimes happens that, for some reason or other, those parents can't keep the child they have had together. Your "new" parents have probably told you already that your birth mom (who was actually very young and on her own by that time) thought it best to put you in a special home where you could be properly looked after until someone adopted you.

In other words, it is impossible.

Wait. Hear me out. What happened next was that people started looking around to see if they could find you new parents. They did. They found these grown-ups who took you into their home, gave you their name, shared their lives with you and became your new family. That's what being an adoptive parent is all about – not simply giving birth to a child, but committing to that child on a lifetime basis. And that's why I think the answer to your question is probably "no". It seems to me that a dad and a mom are best defined as the people who raise a child and spend their lives doing everything they can for him or her. Besides, it would be very difficult for any child to accept that he or she has not one but two sets of parents.

Does that mean that my birth parents don't exist any more?

No, you're not expected simply to "erase" your birth parents from your life. But I think that, little by little, you'll come to think of them in a different way. Exactly *how*, of course, will be for you to decide.

Just because I don't speak about them a lot doesn't mean to say I don't think about them.

There's nothing wrong with that! Nobody believes for a second that an adopted child doesn't think about his or her life before adoption from time to time.

I was quite old when I was adopted. Do younger children think the same way?

Yes, even children who were very young when they were adopted. This is usually because their new parents have taken the time to talk to them about adoption and what it means. Parents know how

important it is that a child understands this – as you
now do – and knows how much he or she is loved.

But I can still think about my birth parents now and then?
Of course. And talking about them is also important.

CHAPTER 8

Where do I come from?

An adopted child's country of origin is an important question that needs to be addressed, both by adoptive parents and adopted children. Where a child originally came from can pose particular problems for parents. They may feel a sense of gratitude towards the adopted child's native country, but this may be tempered by ongoing uncertainty with regard to how – for the child's sake – they should relate to that country in future. Should they talk to the child about it? Should they learn to speak the language of the country concerned? Or should they, at the very least, make sure that the child learns that language? Should they all re-visit the child's birthplace and, if so, how often and when? Clearly, the answers parents find to these questions will impact on and color a child's attitude to the country of his or her birth.

Adopted children, and particularly adolescents, must also come to terms with how they relate to their country of origin. Some continue to feel a strong attachment, and take considerable pride in it, following developments there closely and resenting or reacting strongly to any adverse comments or criticism. Others, by contrast, may want nothing to do with the country where they were born, refusing to learn the language, for example, or showing no inclination to visit. Even those who do visit may return with mixed feelings. Some will have discovered a culture and lifestyle they admire, whereas others, however much they might physically resemble the people they meet there, will be saddened to find they no longer have a language or background in common. Ultimately, however, an adopted child's questions about the country he or she originally came from may simply be another expression of concerns about birth parents.

On a formal note, the issue of dual nationality can also be a concern. In certain countries, children – adopted or otherwise – always retain their original nationality and will be able to carry both passports. A number of countries also require adopting adults to provide information on the children entrusted to them. However legitimate this requirement may be from the perspective of the country in question, it can also prove unsettling for the adoptive parents.

Ernesto (11; originally from Brazil)

I'm confused. It seems to me that I have two native countries.

Don't you think you're confused simply because you were born in another country?

Maybe that's it. Hussein over at the Youth Center says I'm from here and Brazil at the same time. Is that right?

What links you to Brazil is the fact of having Brazilian birth parents. But you're a citizen here because your adoptive parents are from this country. Your skin color has nothing to do with your nationality!

But isn't it important to respect your country of origin?

Of course it is! It's a way of showing respect for other children and other parents from there.

My parents very rarely mention Brazil. Is that because they don't like it there?

I don't think so. Adoptive parents are usually grateful to the country their children came from. In many instances, they were already familiar with it well before they went ahead with the adoption, but what they now want, above all, is for you to get to know and enjoy this country and its culture.

That's true – in fact, I am beginning to feel more like I'm from here now. I'm into the rap, and the rock music, and the movies, and all that kind of thing. Fact is, I don't feel much like talking about Brazil.

That's only natural. Your friend Hussein probably only mentions Brazil because, like you, he was born in another country and now lives in this country with his adoptive parents. To be honest, I don't think it's very helpful at all if the people around you keep referring to where you were born as "your" country. I don't see how that will help you adapt to and fit in with your new surroundings. And, when push comes to shove, I think it should be up to you, and you alone, to decide which country you regard as "your" country.

But then, I'm a big soccer fan, and I support Brazil! It makes me proud when they win!

There's nothing to prevent you liking some things about the country of your birth! Including how good they are at soccer!

Is it true that I can choose my nationality when I'm 18?

Whether or not you can opt for dual nationality depends on the laws of the country of your birth and the law here, so you would need to investigate.

Anne (10; originally from Sri Lanka)

I've seen photographs of where I was born and I have to say I feel lucky I was adopted!

If anyone should feel lucky, then it's your new parents for having had the good fortune to find you! They were so sad because they couldn't have children of their own and they'd been looking to adopt a child for ages! You wouldn't believe how happy they were when they traveled to Sri Lanka to fetch you! But I can understand that you also feel fortunate to have found a new family that loves you.

If you ask me, there are many children in my country who could be adopted. There is so much poverty there!

Now there's a very considerate thought! I know that the country is poor, and that there are many unfortunate children living there. But that isn't a reason for children to be legally available for adoption – not if they still have parents of their own.

Jeremy (10)

There was a big earthquake in the country my little sister comes from, and I've been told many children were left without parents. Don't you think they should all be adopted?

You believe we should step in and help these orphaned children generally?

Why not? It makes sense, if you ask me. Besides, my mom and dad could adopt another child – and that would be a little brother for me!

I agree we should do all we can to help, but I don't think that wholesale adoption is the answer. First of all, these children may have lost their parents but there are probably a lot of other family members still capable of caring for them: grandparents, aunts, uncles, older brothers and sisters, cousins, and so on. What I'm saying is that the children may have been orphaned, but they have *not* necessarily been abandoned. Perhaps the best we can do at such a difficult time is to help the family members who have survived to find one another. Obviously, we should do as much as we can to help clothe and feed people, and to make sure they have a roof over their heads, and even some money.

In fact, it may be that the very last thing we should do is to add to their troubles by uprooting them from their native country. It is important to see that adoption can't resolve such problems – it is not a panacea. I think we should do whatever we can to help out in a crisis by helping the country as a whole, and that will help to take the strain off families and single parents and ensure they are not forced to give up their children. As for providing you with a little brother, that is a matter for your parents to decide.

But there are so many orphans, especially when there's a war going on.

I agree, it's horrible that children should lose their parents, and I understand your concern, but international law specifically prohibits children being given up for adoption in war zones or in countries where a natural disaster has occurred. Among other things, the law is there to prevent trafficking in children and orphans.

But what are we doing for the world's orphans?

We help in other ways. We can make donations to humanitarian organizations, for example. If you like, you could arrange for a collection to be made in your own school, to raise cash to buy books, writing materials, that sort of thing. Adults can also sponsor a child and pledge long-term funding to provide him or her with food and shelter or to help underwrite his or her education.

It's worth repeating that adoption should *never* be regarded as some sort of generalized humanitarian gesture. Instead, it must be a gesture of individual love and commitment, the expression of a heartfelt desire for parenthood. The decision to adopt must be based on mature reflection rather than a reaction to the gruesome images we see all too often on our TV screens.

Maya (11)

It was Maya's parents who brought her to see me.

One day she turned to me and said: *I'm sick of my mom going on and on about Russia and then parading me in front of visitors who say they're also thinking about adopting a Russian girl like me. It's almost as if I'm being held up as some kind of proof that adoption works!*

I asked Maya if she'd ever had a word with her mom about this. She answered that it was "awkward". It transpired that her mother had started a parent association and that Maya didn't want to "rock the boat" by saying something that might give offense.

I asked whether she had mentioned the problem to her dad. She replied: *He's not interested. My mom has nothing but good things to say about Russia, but not him! He never says a word!*

So I then asked Maya what she was planning to do.

One thing's for sure — there's no way I'm going to learn to speak Russian, or even travel to Russia, at least not for the time being! What I want to do is study my favorite subject — mathematics — and get into research some day.

Your mom obviously feels she is doing the right thing and she is clearly anxious to share her own happiness and good fortune with other couples looking to adopt. But if you don't want to be involved, then it's best to make that clear as soon as you can. It's my guess she'll understand, even though she'll probably be disappointed.

CHAPTER 9

Sometimes it's hard to be adopted!

When adopted children "act up" – as the phrase goes – it may be for all sorts of reasons. It follows that a prime duty of parents is to make a concerted effort to understand the underlying cause or causes. Sometimes, an adopted child's patterns of behavior can be sourced to his or her history prior to adoption. There may, on the other hand, be contributory factors that are common to children in general rather than peculiar to adopted children.

In addition to dealing with the obvious logistical problems implicit in removing a child from a familiar environment, country, or language, it is essential to monitor how the adopted child is dealing with the personal history he or she has inherited, or sometimes invented. Equally important, obviously, is the way in which he or she communicates and builds relationships with other people.

In the final analysis, an adopted child is no different from any other child to the extent that children everywhere progress towards maturity via various stages of potentially traumatic physical and psychological development and adjustment. What can color the situation in the case of an adopted child, however, is the specific way he or she perceives adoption *per se*. Is it a major factor in his or her life? Or does the child feel it is of little or no real consequence? Clearly, each adopted child will respond in his or her own individual way, but it is always useful to talk things through as objectively as possible.

Should this prove difficult, parents should not hesitate to involve a third party; they should always bear in mind that asking for help is not a sign of parental incompetence!

Isabel (10)

Dad says he doesn't understand why I'm always so difficult, when my parents were kind enough to adopt me!

What a strange notion! Do you think the fact of being adopted should mean that children have to be on their best behavior day in, day out?

But won't they stop loving me if I misbehave too much?

Whenever you start acting up, it's not hard to see that your parents might be angry with you for a time, but it passes. You can't really blame them for that, can you? In my experience, children who are scolded for doing something wrong often insist that their parents don't love them any more, but, in fact, it is often the children who don't love their parents when they have misbehaved and then been punished or reprimanded. Parents are usually quite reasonable: they don't expect children to be well behaved *all* the time.

My parents wanted a child so much that they now let me do whatever I want!

That could turn out to be the problem! They are so happy to have been able to adopt that you've been permitted to take advantage of the situation – as children often do. But I think it's time you started to think seriously about this, don't you?

Maybe, but it's tough being abandoned, and people think I have it easy!

Can you explain?

People probably think things are okay because I don't say anything.

Possibly, but how can they know what you're thinking? They're not mind readers. And don't you think they might be worried when you start looking sad or preoccupied? Time and again, it all comes down to the same thing – you have to talk to one another! Or are you worried that talking about it might upset your parents in some way?

Yes. I just don't want to talk about it!
I can understand that, but I'm sure your parents would prefer you to confide in them.

So you say, but my dad never replies to any of my questions!
It's not always easy for parents when it comes to answering a child's questions. This is sometimes because they simply don't have an answer and they are embarrassed because they know how important the question may be to the child. Sometimes, it's because they're worried that what they say in reply may be upsetting. And, in some cases, it's because they simply don't understand why the child is asking these questions at all, especially when everything seems to be going along okay. You say your dad never answers your questions: what about your mom?

Oh, yes, she even replies to the questions that I've asked my dad!

Well, it could be that your dad thinks you're asking all these questions because things are not okay with you, and that has worried him. Perhaps you have to choose the moment more carefully and approach him when he is in a mood to reply.

What really bugs me is how they want me to be just like them! But I want to be me!

You *are* you! You have your own distinctive manner and personality, your good points and your bad points, just like everyone else. On the other hand, why wouldn't you want to share some characteristics with your mom and dad? Where's the harm in that? Being like them in some respects won't detract from you as a person in your own right, will it? Or could it be that you resent the fact that they seem to love you a bit *too* much for comfort?

Jonathan (7)

Dad is always saying how much Paul will grow up to look like him.

Sure, Paul will grow up to look like him. Or like your mom. Or maybe a bit like both of them. Who knows? Does it matter?

But I'll still be theirs, won't I, even now that Paul's around?

Of course! A lot of adopted children ask that question at one time or another and, in almost every instance, they end up by supplying the answer themselves. It is understandable that there's a risk of jealousy: you're probably a little jealous right now. But your parents will always think of both you and your little brother as their children, no matter that you came into their lives in different ways. They've now made room in their hearts for Paul just as they once made a special place in their hearts for you. In other words, there's more than enough love for both of you.

Mom says I'm still her little baby!

Is that what you want?

Why not? That way, she'll always be there to take care of me!

You're right in one way – a little baby needs so much more attention than the likes of you, a big boy of seven who is old enough and smart enough to do things for himself. I wonder how your parents feel about that? Don't you think they might prefer having a big boy of seven rather than two little babies? And ask yourself how you'd feel about being back in a pushchair and sucking on a comforter?

Maybe that would be fun for a while.

Is that so? But only for a while, eh?

Well, yes. Not all the time, of course.

I see. Only when it suits you, perhaps?

Gabriel (8)

I'm sick of having two birthdays!

Do you mean that your parents celebrate both your actual birthday and the day you were adopted?

Yes.

But which would *you* rather have?

I'd like to have just one birthday and one birthday party for myself and my friends! Just like everyone else!

If that's how you feel, you must tell your parents. Adopting you was a wonderful and happy experience for them, but that's *their* anniversary and, if they feel like celebrating, perhaps they should celebrate with one another.

And what about Grandma? Don't you think she should ask me if it's okay with me before she tells someone I'm adopted?

In principle, I really agree with you on that one! Of course, I don't know what prompted your grandma to tell someone that you are an adopted child, but what I *do* know is that you've every right to ask her why. And you could explain to her that you think that it's your business, and that you would rather discuss it if and when you feel like it.

Lydia (10)

If I told them how I really feel right now, I don't think my parents would love me any more. I want to find my real mom!

That's a tough one! The first thing to do is to clarify what you really want to find out, and I have to warn you that it could take some time! As for your parents not loving you any more, I find that hard to believe, whatever you may say. They are there for you and you can always tell them what's on your mind, and trust them to understand.

Could you maybe talk to them with me?

I'm more than happy to help all three of you tackle questions like these. I know they can be difficult and I'm always ready to help if I can.

Catherine (11)

Maria is quite different from the rest of us!

That's true, but not only because she's adopted. She is also handicapped – physically disabled, as we say today.

But why did Mom and Dad want to adopt her in that case? Why didn't someone else take care of her?

Your parents adopted her quite simply because they wanted to very much and didn't mind that she had health problems. They probably thought that every child has a right to a home and a family. And, since you are almost grown-up already, they probably thought you would welcome a little sister into the family, and help care for her as she grows up, handi-capped or not.

But you didn't answer my question: why didn't someone else take care of her?

Perhaps that wasn't an option in the country where she was born – maybe there were no facilities or maybe it was simply too expensive. But you'll see: she'll be given the best medical treatment in this country, and things will turn out really well for her.

Gina (11)

Things aren't going well at school right now, but I don't feel I can talk to my mom about it.

You'll need to be more specific so that I can help.

I overheard the substitute teacher ask my mom if I have these problems because I'm adopted.

There are many children who have problems at school and it's got nothing to do with whether or not they're adopted. But I have spoken to your mom about this and she tells me you didn't attend pre-school back in your country.

Maybe, maybe not. I don't remember.

That doesn't surprise me – it was all so long ago. Your mom says there was no school where you lived then, and it wasn't until you came to this country that you went to school for the first time. By then, you were six years old.

Is that why I've been sent here to see you?

No, you're only here because you seem to have some questions that are bothering you. And there's absolutely nothing wrong with that: asking questions and looking for answers is all part of growing up. It's simply healthy curiosity.

You're right. I am curious, mainly because my friend Anna keeps asking me questions about where I used to live, how come I was adopted, who my real parents are, that sort of thing. And I don't know what I'm supposed to reply.

Why haven't you told your parents about this?

Because I don't want to upset them: Mom especially. The last time I brought up stuff like that, I could tell how upset she was. At the same time, I'd still like to know what I should say to Anna!

I think we should *both* talk this through with your mom. That way, things should sort themselves out pretty quickly: it will help clear the air – for you both!

Francis (13)

What happens if adoption doesn't work out? Or if it turns out we don't like one another?

Are you thinking of anyone in particular?

I guess so. My best friend isn't getting along with his parents. And it's been at least five years since he was adopted!

In that case, it appears we're up against a real problem. I don't have an answer right off the top of my head. All I can say is that you can't switch love on and off at will. It's an emotion that has to build gradually as people get to know and understand one another. That goes for parents and children alike, and you can bet your life it holds true for your friend's parents. I don't doubt for an instant that they are doing their best in the circumstances. What you – and your friend – have to accept is that some children need more time than others to adjust and to learn how to trust – and love – those who have shown good faith as adoptive parents. Things get more complicated, I freely admit, if – for one reason or another – the adopted child does not "come up to expectations".

What happens then?

There's no easy answer. In my experience, merely talking things over rarely does any good. It's best to seek specialist advice and help. Even then, there are no guarantees. All that I can say now is that it's a mistake to let a situation like that get out of hand and drag on indefinitely. Instead, something needs to be done about it as soon as possible.

Natalie (8; originally from Russia)

I have an older brother and a little sister back in the country where I was born. I'd like to know where they are now.

How did you find out about them in the first place?

There's this lady I know – a friend of my parents – who told us about my brother and sister. But I remember them myself.

Remember what exactly?

I remember all of us playing together when we were in the orphanage. Do you think I could see them again some day or maybe write to them?

That's not for me to say; it's up to your parents to decide what's best in this situation. All I can suggest is that I'll help you bring the subject up with them, if you'd like that and if they agree. What you and I can talk about are your memories, what you imagine about that time, and what you think you would like to do. I know that thinking about your brother and sister raises lots of questions, and I'm afraid there's nothing I can do about that.

Angelica (15; originally from Cyprus)

I've just found out about my sister. She's living with different parents back home in Cyprus. We've e-mailed one another already.

That must make you happy.

Yes, it does. I'm really glad I know what happened to her. To be honest, it also scares me a little, because we don't really know one another. Still, I suppose writing to one another will help. And another thing: our parents say it'll be okay for us to get together one of these days.

You'd like that?

Yes, and my parents say they'll help.

CHAPTER 10

What about
when
I grow up?

What adopted children have in common with children everywhere is that, sooner or later, they all become adolescents and develop a history of their own. At that juncture, adoptive parents can expect to field some particularly awkward questions, which typically touch on fundamental issues relating to the child's origins and early life. This will include the facts and motives behind his or her adoption, and the potential problems that may arise. As a rule, this is a time when the adolescent will not hesitate to push his adoptive parents to the limit, testing their love and commitment. It is as well to be prepared.

Matthew (10)

Dad says my big brother Paolo is a really difficult teenager!

Adolescence is just a phase. It's a stage we all go through, when we're between childhood and adulthood. Paolo is simply trying to assert his individuality and his independence. That's never easy.

But you think it's normal, how he and Dad argue all the time?

It happens, believe me, and it's got nothing to do with whether one is adopted or not! The stage Paolo is going through right now is often called "teenage rebellion". Basically, it's when adolescents start forming their own opinions about the world and its values. That's normal and it's all part and parcel of growing up. More often than not a teenager's attitude to life seems to clash with that of his or her parents. Paolo is merely trying to find himself, to make his own way in life, and that's why he and your parents – your dad especially – seem to be arguing all the time.

That must be making life difficult for my dad?

I guess so, because he must be having a hard time dealing with Paolo's bid for independence. Besides, your dad may be saddened and hurt by the gap that seems to be opening up between Paolo and himself. Dads have feelings too, remember.

Okay. But if all teenagers go through this, why should it be more difficult for those who are adopted?

Because standing on your own two feet and going it alone can be a scary business at the best of times. For an adopted child, it can also re-awaken the old fears, such as that of being abandoned and left alone again. Going it alone also means precisely that: learning to deal on your own with a new set of problems. And

then there's something else: when you rebel against your parents there is always the fear of losing their love, and perhaps Paolo should also keep that in mind!

Is that what is happening with Paolo?

No, not in any real sense. Your parents love him as much as ever, even though he's giving them a really hard time at the moment. What's more, don't you think they have every right to be irritated and annoyed by his behavior? Fortunately, they know it's just a phase he's going through.

Parents are unlikely to turn against a young child or a teenager just because he or she is being difficult. They know they have to be patient and not demand too much of their teenage children.

So what do you think we should do for the best?

It's always good to talk to one another or to a third party. Teenagers have so much on their minds and there are so many unanswered questions that can cause them anxiety.

My aunt says Paolo would be better off at boarding school.

She may have a point, but it's not her decision. It's for your parents to determine what's best in this situation.

She says she's worried because Paolo suddenly keeps saying he wants to visit his birth parents!

That impulse is not at all uncommon during adolescence. It's not exactly clear *why* Paolo should suddenly feel so strongly about this, but it's important to sit down together and talk about it. Does he genuinely want to meet up with his birth parents? Maybe he wants to visit and get to know the country where he was born. This all leads us to ask how much he already knows or has been told about that country.

Paolo is obviously very confused at present, but this is far from uncommon in a teenager, and it is important that his parents remember to stand together and present a united front.

Adolescence certainly doesn't sound like much fun!

Like your brother Paolo, adolescents tend to need constant reassurance. They need to know their parents still love and understand them, but at the same time they don't want their parents to suffocate them by being on top of them. What they need is not so much constant attention, but freedom and space to do their own thing and grow up in their own way. In the process, both parents and children will have to come to terms with the fact that, although they will continue to love one another, their love will find different forms of expression as time goes by.

CHAPTER 11

Will I be able to adopt a child when I grow up?

As adopted children get older, they generally start asking various other questions about their own future. This is particularly true of young girls, who are predictably intrigued by the prospect of motherhood and all that it implies. They are understandably anxious to learn if they too can bear children and often ask whether or not they may also one day adopt children.

Such questions are perfectly natural and reflect no more than a continuing preoccupation on the part of children with their family history and their ongoing relationship with their adoptive parents and an image of their biological parents that they may have either retained or imagined.

Sophia (14)

Will I be able to adopt children, eventually?

When the time comes and you're old enough, of course you'll be able to have children of your own, either in the usual way or by way of adoption! You must do as your own parents did, however, which is to think long and hard before taking the first step towards adoption. You should be clear in your own mind as to *why* you feel the need to adopt.

Do all adopted children go on to adopt children of their own when they grow up?

Not in my experience. Some will grow up and be content to have children in the conventional way, whereas others will have children of their own and also adopt, and others will have no children of their own and may want to adopt. It all depends on their individual circumstances. Someone who has been an adopted child and has had a happy childhood, with a good relationship with his or her parents, might quite naturally feel a wish to relive that experience with an adopted child. Let's face it, that's as good a way as any other of passing things on from one generation to the next.

Rick (10)

My mom was adopted, but she had my brother and me with our dad. What I would like to know is if our grandma is really our grandma?

Of course she is. Your grandma is your mom's mom. Although she didn't physically give birth to your mom, she and her husband – your grandad – cherished her, named her, cared for her, and put her through school and college. You tell me, what could be more "real" than that?

A checklist for children

- Birth parents do not abandon children because they are ugly or unattractive, but because they do not have the means to care for them.

- Parents adopt because they have a strong desire to have children.

- In order to adopt a child, parents have to commit themselves in writing.

- Parents are not permitted to select a child, nor can a child select his or her parents.

- To be adopted, children must be declared "legally available for adoption".

- Children available for adoption live temporarily in institutions, special homes, or nurseries, or, in some cases, with foster parents.

- Children can be adopted at any age. Age is not a barrier to adoption.

- Children can *never* be bought or sold.

- Adoption is governed by national and international laws, which have been passed specifically to safeguard the rights of both children and parents.

- Family "resemblance" is not only physical. A child can be "like" his or her dad or mom even when they are not the child's birth parents.

- Children need, and deserve, to be told the truth at all times.

- It is important to tell children as much as possible of what is known about their past.

- Children of the same parents are "brothers" and "sisters", even when the parents are not their birth or biological parents.

- At first, a child may feel jealous towards a new arrival in the family, but should always remember that parents have enough love in their hearts to share with all their children.

- An adopted child may have several first names, including those given to him or her at birth and those chosen for him or her by his adoptive parents.

- Children are always free to ask their adoptive parents questions about their birth parents or about the country of their birth.

- Children cannot be adopted in war zones or areas of natural disaster.

- Adoption is not to be confused with a humanitarian gesture towards children living in poverty, not least if they still have a family of their own.

- Adoption is a private matter and there is no obligation to discuss it with all and sundry.

- Adoption is not always easy for children.

- Adoption is a very beautiful idea.

A note for parents only

The act of adoption creates a permanent bond between parents and children. Irrespective of how much the one may know about the other, however, and no matter how effectively that information is transmitted, there will inevitably be a number of unknown factors to contend with.

To the adopted child, such unknowns can assume particular importance: they are effectively holes in the fabric of the child's personal history. It is in order to plug those holes that adopted children tend to ask so many questions of themselves and of their parents. Parents need to accept that one "catch-all" response is never sufficient; their children will keep right on asking questions over and over until they are satisfied with the reply. Through their answers, parents should be trying to help their children develop a sense of their shared identity. It follows that each and every question a child asks should be taken seriously and answered calmly and with authority.

We all know that, ultimately, no parent will ever come up with the perfect responses. That may not always be such a bad thing: children need to know that their parents don't always have all the answers!

The 1989 Convention on the Rights of the Child is a legally binding international instrument. It makes provision in its articles and protocols for the full range of children's rights, including the right to survival, to develop to the fullest potential, to be protected against harm, abuse, and exploitation, and to participate fully in family, cultural, and social life. The Convention protects these rights by setting standards in health care, education, and legal, civil, and social services. Articles 20 and 21 relate specifically to adoption and the duties and obligations of competent national authorities.

Detailed provisions with respect to adoption across national frontiers are set out in the Convention on Inter-Country Adoption signed in The Hague in 1993. The Hague Convention makes provision, *inter alia*, for rules outlawing trafficking in children. Not all countries are signatories, but visiting www.hcch.net/index_en.php will give details and a full text.

Useful websites

There are a very large number of potentially useful sites, of which the following is simply a selection. Because adoption is now international in its nature, there are a number of sites that offer information globally.

www.iss-ssi.org

> The International Social Service (ISS) is an international non-governmental organization dedicated to helping individuals and families with personal or social problems resulting from migration and international movement. Adoption is one of the issues with which the ISS is involved.

http://international.adoption.com

> A US based organization with links to worldwide adoption facilities.

United States

www.nacac.org

> North American Council on Adoptable Children . The NACAC promotes and supports permanent families for children and youths in the US and Canada who have been in care—especially those in foster care and those with special needs.

www.davethomasfoundation.org

> The Dave Thomas Foundation for Adoption is a nonprofit public charity dedicated to dramatically increasing the adoptions of the more than 140,000 children in North America's foster care systems waiting to be adopted.

www.childwelfare.gov/nfcad

> The National Foster Care & Adoption Directory (formerly the National Adoption Directory) offers adoption and foster care resources by state.

www.adoptivefamilies.com

> Publication focusing on adoptive and prospective adoptive families.

www.adopting.com

> A website offering references to adoption organizations and charities.

United Kingdom

www.adoption.org.uk

> Site offering general information and a directory of adoption agencies in the UK.

www.adoptionuk.org

> A registered charity and self-help group.

www.dfes.gov.uk/intercountryadoption

> Official site for information on adoption from other countries and the pertaining law in the UK and elsewhere.

www.everychildmatters.gov.uk/adoption

> Official site with practical and legal details.

www.direct.gov.uk/en/Parents/Adoptionfosteringandchildren
incare
Official site with details of public services.

www.baaf.org.uk
Site for the British Association for Adoption & Fostering.

Canada

www.canadiancrc.com
A nonprofit, non-governmental educational and
advocacy organization dedicated to supporting the rights
and responsibilities of Canadian children.

www.children.gov.on.ca/mcys/english/programs/child/
adoption
An official site, run by the Government of Ontario.

www.adoption.ca
The Adoption Council of Canada (ACC) is the umbrella
organization for adoption in Canada.

Australia

www.australia.gov.au/Birth,_Adoption,_Marriage,_Divorce,_Etc.
Government site covering all aspects of family law, and
offering links to state law and international adoption.

www.adoptionaustralia.org
An adoption forum site.

New Zealand

www.cyf.govt.nz/adoptions.htm
Site offering official information on adoption.